50 Creative Minecraft Writing Prompts

Written by Hannah Evans

50 Creative Minecraft Writing Prompts

Written and illustrated by Hannah Evans

Ignite your youngsters passion
for writing by giving
them this fun and creative
Minecraft writing prompt book! They will create
their own stories, comics, pictures and color fun
original pictures.

THE PURPOSE OF A WRITING PROMPT IS TO INVITE STUDENTS TO THINK ABOUT, DEVELOP A PERSPECTIVE AND WRITE ABOUT A TOPIC. FINISH THESE STORIES WITH YOUR OWN WORDS. USE BOTH SIDES OF THE BRAIN WITH THIS BOOK WHILE WRITING, CREATING COMICS, ILLUSTRATING YOUR STORY AND COLORING PICTURES.

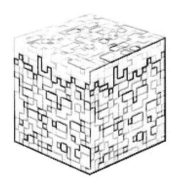 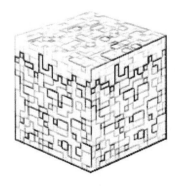 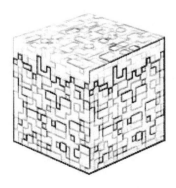

STEVE INVITES YOU TO COME HANG OUT IN HIS UNDER-GROUND LIVING QUARTERS WHEN SUDDENLY OUT OF THE CORNER OF YOUR EYE, STANDS SOMETHING YOU HAVE NEVER SEEN BEFORE...

_____

_____

_____

_____

_____

_____

_____

_____

_____

_____

DRAW A PICTURE TO GO WITH YOUR STORY.

ALEX IS HAVING A GARDEN PARTY WITH YOU AND THREE OF YOUR BEST FRIENDS. HER GARDEN IS FULL OF YUMMY VEGETABLES FOR EVERYONE. SHE PLANS...

_____

_____

_____

_____

_____

_____

_____

_____

_____

_____

WHAT IS THE MOST DETAILED THING YOU HAVE EVER CREATED IN YOUR WORLD?

_____

_____

_____

_____

_____

_____

_____

_____

_____

_____

CREATE A COMIC ABOUT YOUR STORY.

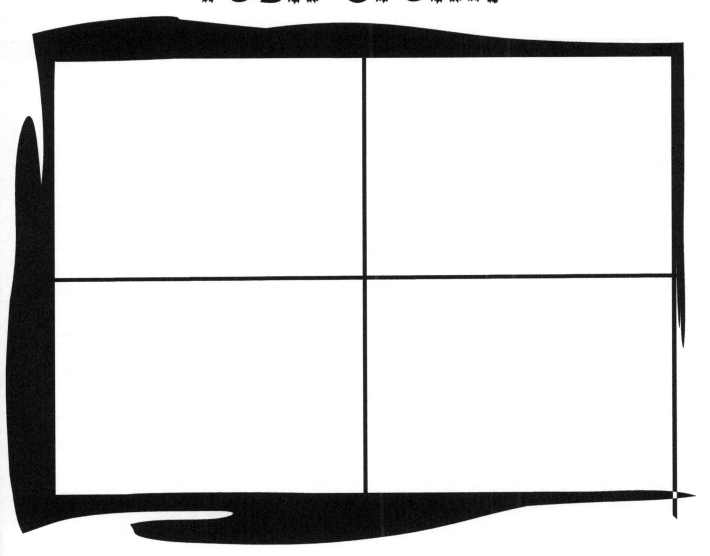

ENDERMAN IS CLOSE TO THE VILLAGE. AS SOON AS YOU START TO WARN THE VILLAGERS THE MOST UNUSUAL THING HAPPENS...

_____

_____

_____

_____

_____

_____

_____

_____

_____

_____

DRAW A PICTURE TO GO WITH YOUR STORY.

WHILE MINING FOR PRECIOUS RESOURCES YOU REALIZE HUGE SPIDERS ARE COMING...

_____

_____

_____

_____

_____

_____

_____

_____

_____

_____

_____

THE MAKERS OF MINECRAFT CALL AND ASK YOU TO COME WORK FOR THE COMPANY TO IMPROVE MINECRAFT. THEY ASK YOU FOR HELP...

_____

_____

_____

_____

_____

_____

_____

_____

_____

_____

CREATE A COMIC ABOUT YOUR STORY.

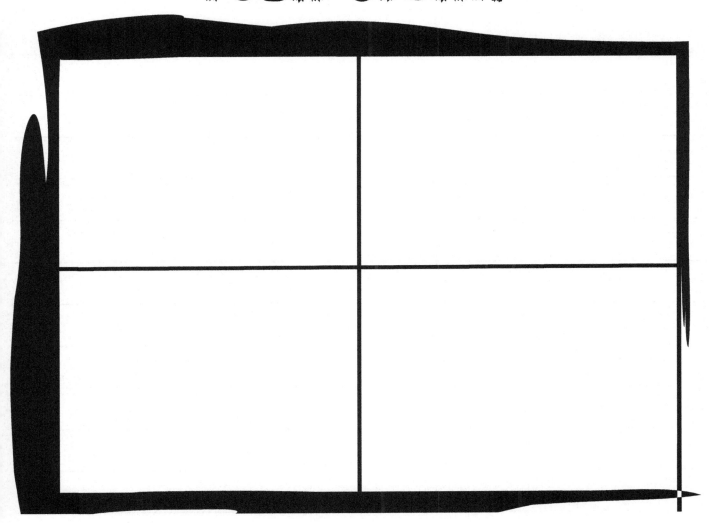

YOUR WORLD WAS DELETED AND YOU MUST REBUILD THE WORLD. YOU START REBUILDING THE...

_____

_____

_____

_____

_____

_____

_____

_____

_____

_____

DRAW A PICTURE TO GO WITH YOUR STORY.

YOU FIND ANOTHER GAMER WONDERING AROUND YOUR HOUSE. HE DROPPED A CHEST AND INSIDE...

_____

_____

_____

_____

_____

_____

_____

_____

_____

_____

_____

YOU WAKE UP TO FIND THE COOLEST MINECRAFT CREATURE LIVING IN YOUR ROOM WITH YOU...

_____

_____

_____

_____

_____

_____

_____

_____

_____

_____

CREATE A COMIC ABOUT YOUR STORY.

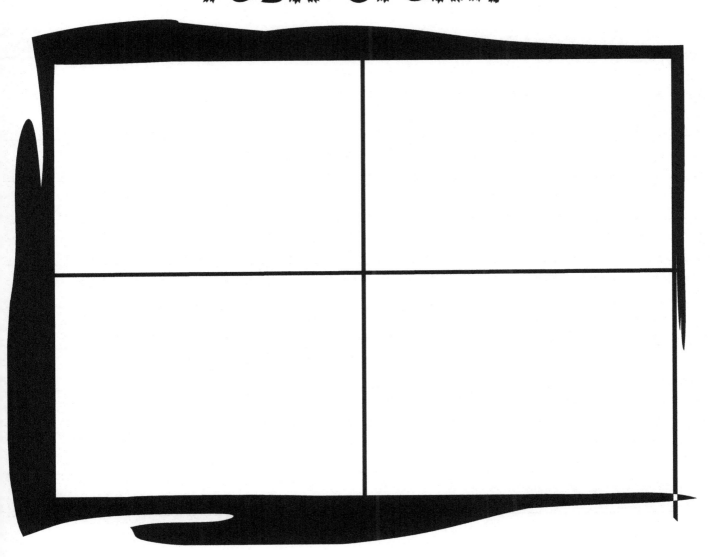

WHILE MINING FOR ORE YOU SEE SOMETHING SPARKLING AND IT CATCHES YOUR EYE, YOU DECIDE TO CHECK IT OUT AND DISCOVER. . .

_____

_____

_____

_____

_____

_____

_____

_____

_____

_____

_____

DRAW A PICTURE TO GO WITH YOUR STORY.

Steve was foraging for wild vegetables in the forest to create a delicious meal. Unfortunately, tonight he...

_____

_____

_____

_____

_____

_____

_____

_____

_____

_____

YOU ARE OUT LOOKING FOR A NEW LOCATION TO BUILD YOUR HOME. WHILE SEARCHING FOR THE PERFECT PLACE YOU COME ACROSS. . ..

_____

_____

_____

_____

_____

_____

_____

_____

_____

_____

CREATE A COMIC ABOUT YOUR STORY.

You live in a big beautiful castle on an island. Describe this island and castle in detail.

_____

_____

_____

_____

_____

_____

_____

_____

_____

_____

DRAW A PICTURE TO GO WITH YOUR STORY.

PERSUADE A VILLAGER THAT YOU HAVE BEEN HELPING TO LET YOU LIVE IN HIS HOUSE FOR THE NIGHT.

_____

_____

_____

_____

_____

_____

_____

_____

_____

_____

CREATE A COMIC ABOUT YOUR STORY.

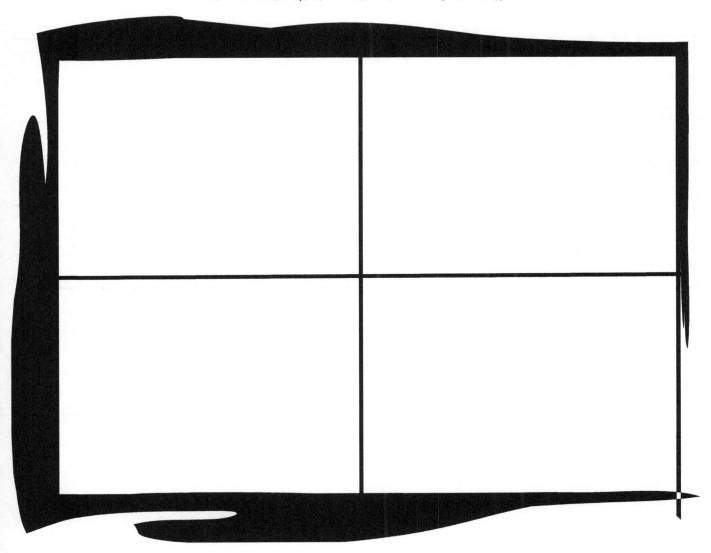

WHILE EXPLORING THE VILLAGE YOU FIND A STRANGE ANIMAL...

_____

_____

_____

_____

_____

_____

_____

_____

_____

_____

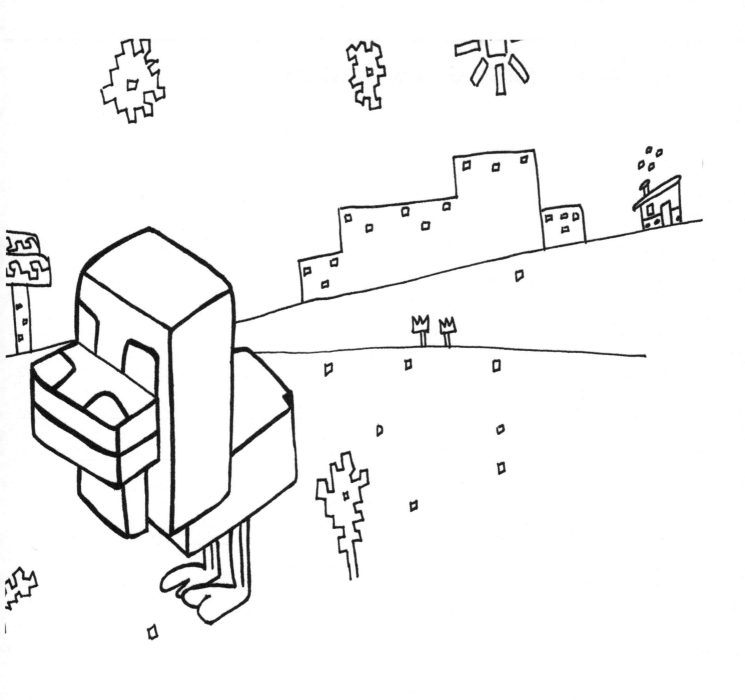

DanTDM IS CHASING YOU BECAUSE...

_____

_____

_____

_____

_____

_____

_____

_____

_____

_____

DRAW A PICTURE TO GO WITH YOUR STORY.

You are exploring the underground when you come across a chest. You see shadows on the walls. You open it when suddenly...

_____

_____

_____

_____

_____

_____

_____

_____

_____

_____

You're digging in the garden and find a fist-sized nugget of gold. You must find out if there is more gold so you...

_____

_____

_____

_____

_____

_____

_____

_____

_____

_____

CREATE A COMIC ABOUT YOUR STORY.

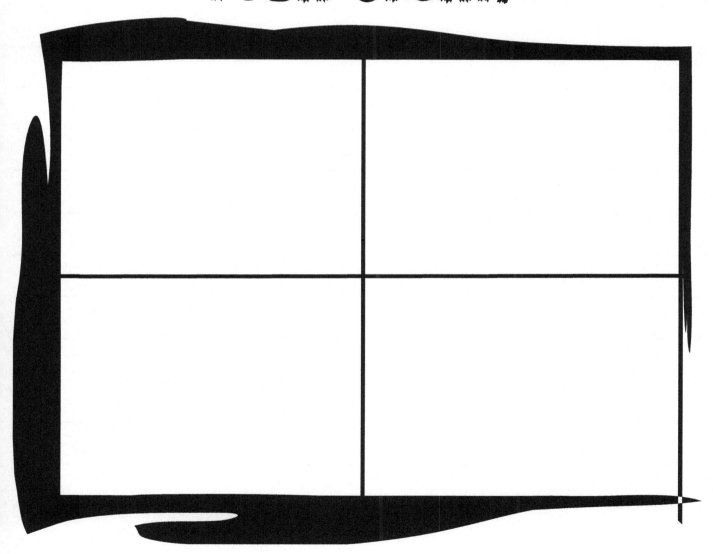

It is night, you are in your house. Creepers are surrounding your house. Fearing they might blow your house up or knock down your door, you need to act fast. Your first action is:

_____

_____

_____

_____

_____

_____

_____

_____

_____

_____

_____

_____

DRAW A PICTURE TO GO WITH YOUR STORY.

STEVE HAS PUT YOU IN CHARGE FOR THE DAY OF CREATING YOUR FAVORITE RESTAURANTS IN THE VILLAGE. WHAT RESTAURANTS ARE YOU BUILDING? WHAT KIND OF FOOD DO THEY SERVE?

_____

_____

_____

_____

_____

_____

_____

_____

_____

_____

_____

You are lost in the middle of the sea. Millions of fish are surrounding you. Your health bar is low, you are almost dead so you decide to...

_____

_____

_____

_____

_____

_____

_____

_____

_____

_____

CREATE A COMIC ABOUT YOUR STORY.

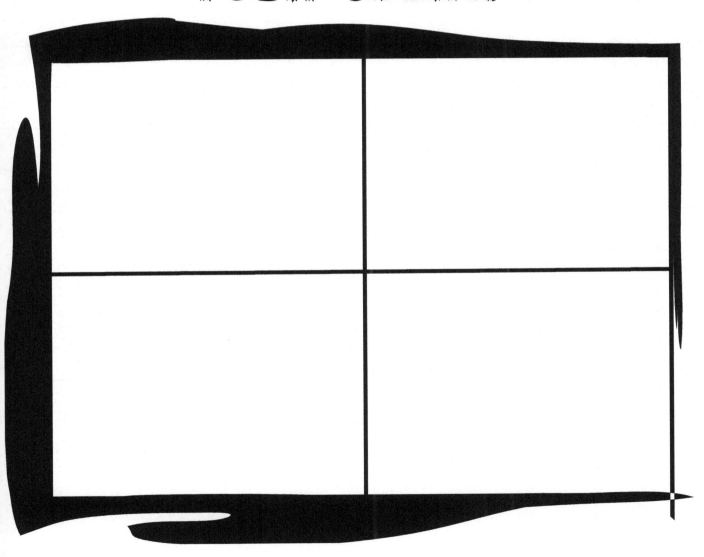

YOU HAVE CREATED YOUR HOME AND NOW YOU NEED TO CREATE A GARDEN. WHERE WILL YOU START YOUR GARDEN? WHAT WILL YOU GROW? WHAT DOES YOUR GARDEN LOOK LIKE? HOW BIG IS IT?

_____

_____

_____

_____

_____

_____

_____

_____

_____

_____

DRAW A PICTURE TO GO WITH YOUR STORY.

It is 2045 in Minecraft. The future is upon us. It's a whole new world. Describe the difference.

_____

_____

_____

_____

_____

_____

_____

_____

_____

_____

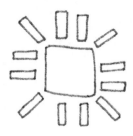

YOU ARE CREATING A JUNGLE TEMPLE. YOU NEED TO CREATE BOOBY TRAPS. WHAT KINDS OF TRAPS WILL YOU MAKE?

_____

_____

_____

_____

_____

_____

_____

_____

_____

_____

CREATE A COMIC ABOUT YOUR STORY.

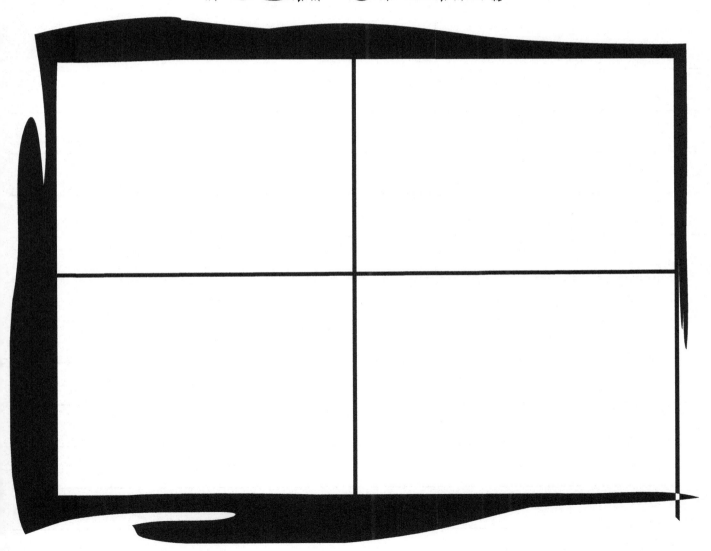

SUDDENLY WATER IS SURROUNDING YOUR.....

_____

_____

_____

_____

_____

_____

_____

_____

_____

_____

_____

DRAW A PICTURE TO GO WITH YOUR STORY.

YOU CAN BUILD A HOME ANYWHERE IN MINECRAFT.
WHERE WILL YOU BUILD YOUR HOME? WILL IT BE TEM-
PORARY OR PERMANENT? WHAT MAKES THIS PLACE SO
SPECIAL?

_____

_____

_____

_____

_____

_____

_____

_____

_____

_____

YOU WALK TO THE VILLAGE LIBRARY WANTING TO FIND A GOOD BOOK. YOU FINALLY FIND THE PERFECT BOOK ABOUT......

_____

_____

_____

_____

_____

_____

_____

_____

_____

_____

_____

CREATE A COMIC ABOUT YOUR STORY.

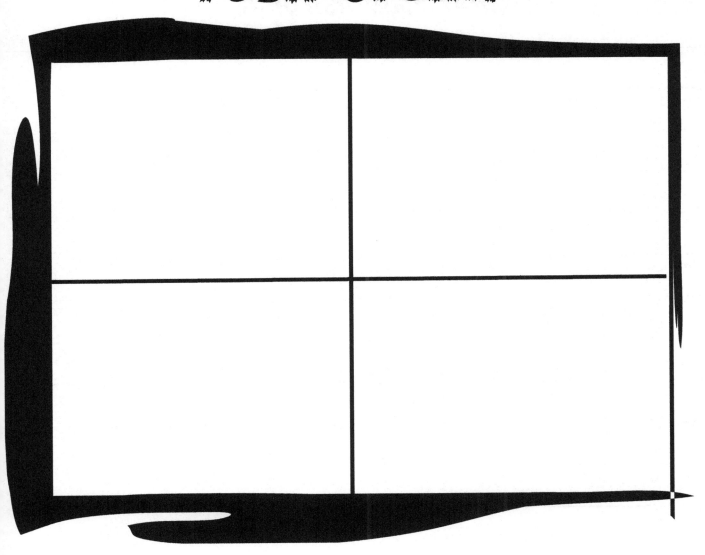

IN ADDITION TO HUTS, HOUSES AND FARMS, VILLAGES HAVE SEVERAL SPECIALIZED BUILDINGS. YOU HAVE BEEN PUT IN CHARGE OF DESIGNING ONE. WHAT ARE YOU BUILDING? DESCRIBE YOUR BUILDING.

_____

_____

_____

_____

_____

_____

_____

_____

_____

_____

DRAW A PICTURE TO GO WITH YOUR STORY.

Villages have a hard time surviving a zombie attack. How would you prevent the zombies from attacking the village? Why is a village important to you in the game?

_____

_____

_____

_____

_____

_____

_____

_____

_____

_____

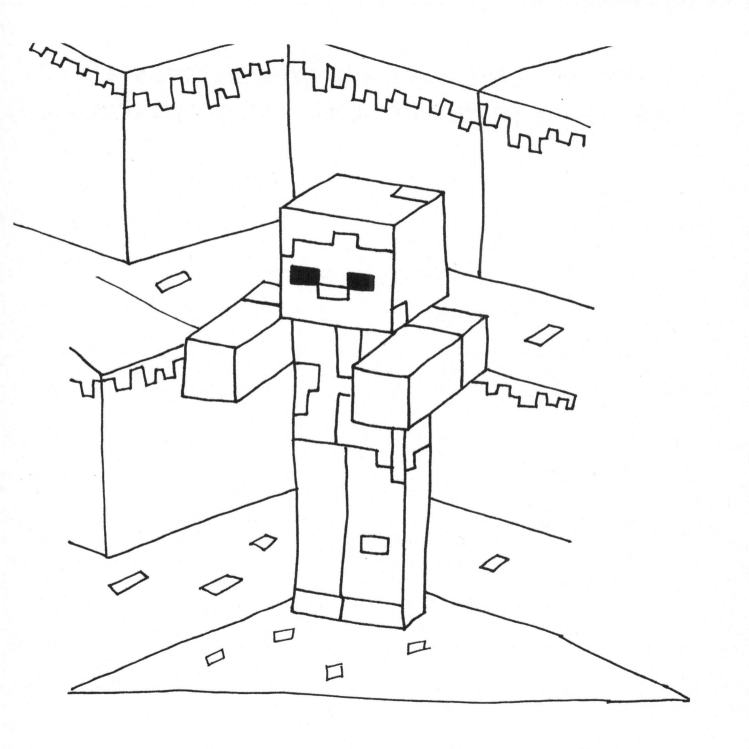

YOU ARE IN A CAVE WHEN YOU STUMBLE UPON A DUNGEON. THE DUNGEON IS DARK, YOU SEE SOMETHING...

_____

_____

_____

_____

_____

_____

_____

_____

_____

_____

_____

CREATE A COMIC ABOUT YOUR STORY.

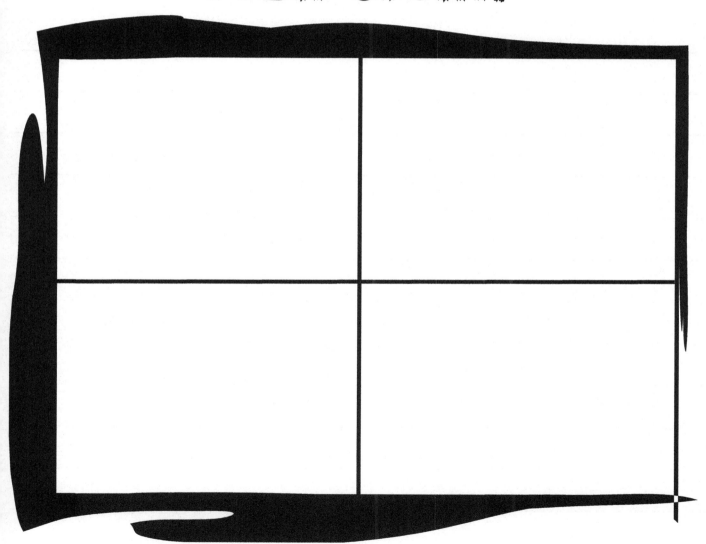

What is your favorite feature in Minecraft? Why? What makes it so special?

_____

_____

_____

_____

_____

_____

_____

_____

_____

_____

_____

_____

DRAW A PICTURE TO GO WITH YOUR STORY.

You see a farm of animals in the distance. You arrive at the farm. The farmer says....

_____

_____

_____

_____

_____

_____

_____

_____

_____

_____

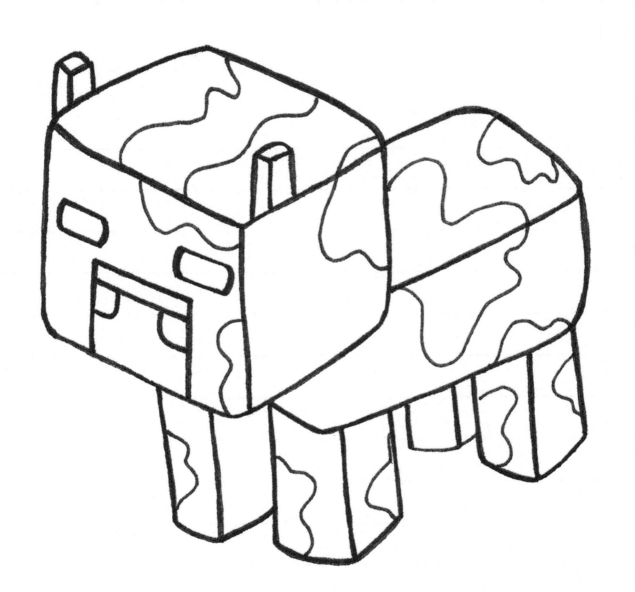

The real world is suddenly turning into Minecraft. . ..

_____

_____

_____

_____

_____

_____

_____

_____

_____

_____

CREATE A COMIC ABOUT YOUR STORY.

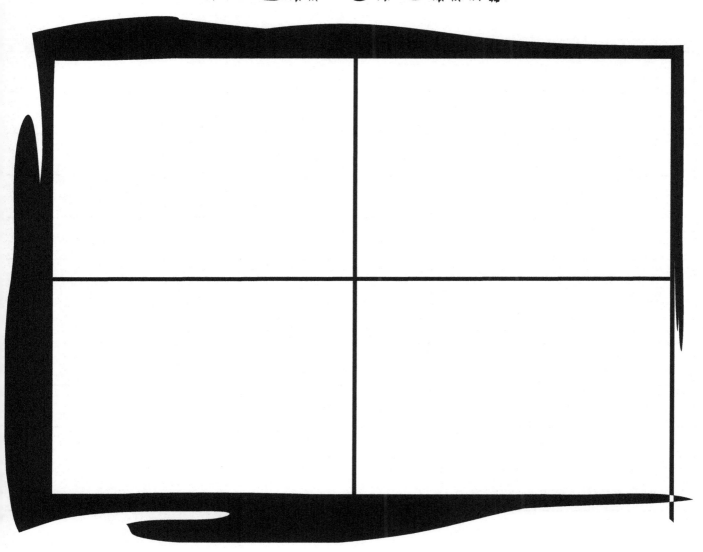

YOU HAVE JUST STUMBLED UPON A RESOURCE YOU HAVE NEVER SEEN BEFORE. WHAT IT IS? WHAT'S IT USED FOR? EXPLAIN IT IN DETAIL.

_____

_____

_____

_____

_____

_____

_____

_____

_____

_____

DRAW A PICTURE TO GO WITH YOUR STORY.

You are playing in survival mode, creepers are surrounding your house. You must. . .

_____

_____

_____

_____

_____

_____

_____

_____

_____

_____

WHAT IS YOUR LEAST FAVORITE THING ABOUT MINECRAFT? WHY? WHAT WOULD YOU CHANGE ABOUT IT?

_____

_____

_____

_____

_____

_____

_____

_____

_____

_____

CREATE A COMIC ABOUT YOUR STORY.

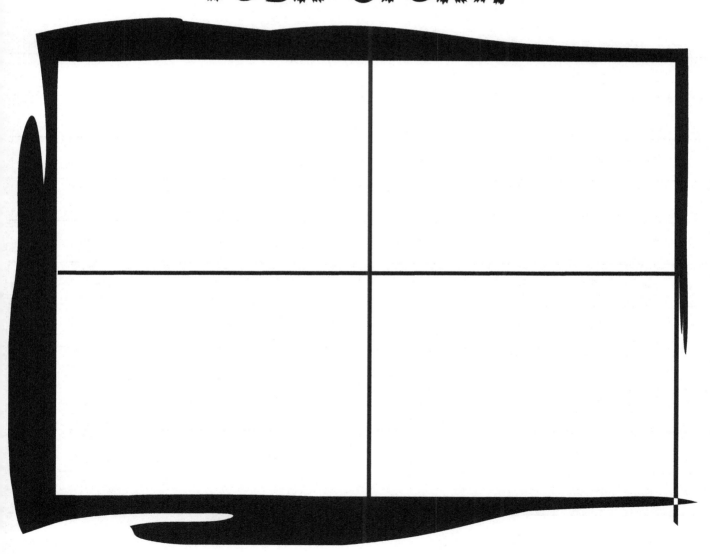

IF CAN ADD ANYTHING TO MINECRAFT WHAT WOULD IT BE AND WHY?

_____

_____

_____

_____

_____

_____

_____

_____

_____

_____

_____

DRAW A PICTURE TO GO WITH YOUR STORY.

YOU HAVE BEEN HIRED TO BUILD A ZOO. DESCRIBE THE ENCLOSURE YOU WILL BUILD. WHAT KIND OF ANIMALS WILL IT HOUSE?

_____

_____

_____

_____

_____

_____

_____

_____

_____

_____

_____

Do you prefer playing Minecraft in Survival mode or Creative mode? Why?

_____

_____

_____

_____

_____

_____

_____

_____

_____

_____

CREATE A COMIC ABOUT YOUR STORY.

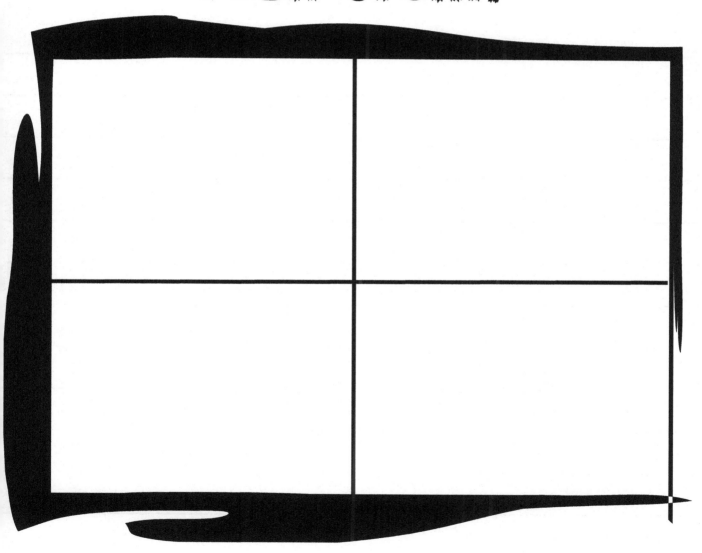

IT'S TIME TO DECORATE YOUR MINECRAFT HOUSE! WHAT STRUCTURAL FEATURES DO YOU WANT TO INCLUDE, SUCH AS WOOD FLOORS OR A GLASS ROOF.

_____

_____

_____

_____

_____

_____

_____

_____

_____

_____

DRAW A PICTURE TO GO WITH YOUR STORY.

As a Minecraft crop farmer, you're getting tired of the same three vegitables. If you could sow three new crops, what will you grow and how will you harvest them?

_____

_____

_____

_____

_____

_____

_____

_____

_____

_____

_____

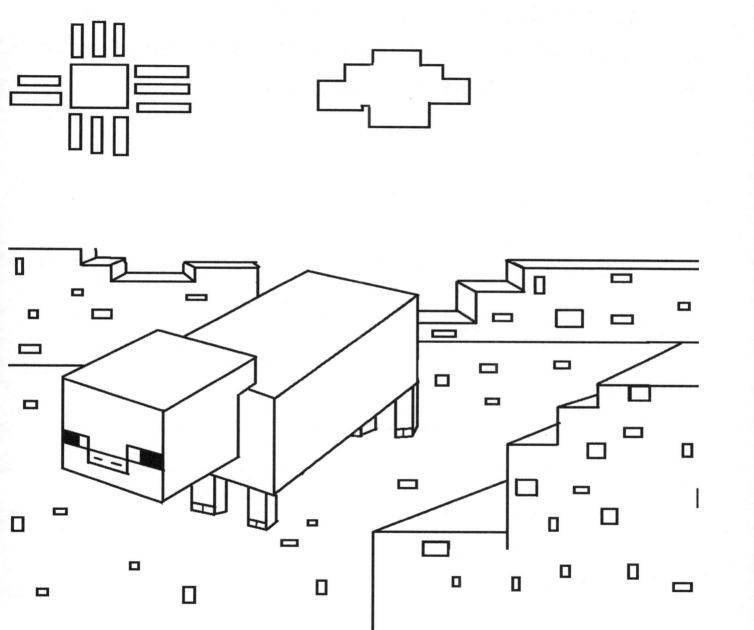

WOULD YOU RATHER BUILD A CASTLE, A TREE HOUSE, OR A BRIDGE? DESCRIBE THE MINECRAFT TOOLS, MATERIALS, AND SUPPLIES YOU WILL USE.

_____

_____

_____

_____

_____

_____

_____

_____

_____

_____

CREATE A COMIC ABOUT YOUR STORY.

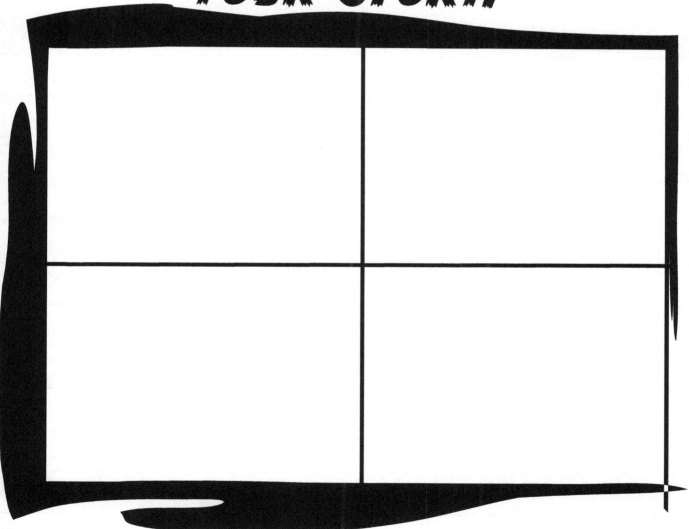

Use your imagination to design a Minecraft building such as a house, mansion, or store. What will you design? Explain in detail.

_____

_____

_____

_____

_____

_____

_____

_____

_____

_____

_____

DRAW A PICTURE TO GO WITH YOUR STORY.

After a horrible shipwreck, you find yourself stranded. You don't know where you are, and it will soon be dark, what will you do first?

_____

_____

_____

_____

_____

_____

_____

_____

_____

_____

_____

YOUR GRANDMA HAS NEVER HEARD OF MINECRAFT. SHE HAS ASKED YOU TO HELP HER UNDERSTAND IT. WRITE A LETTER EXPLAINING WHAT MINECRAFT IS AND WHY YOU ENJOY PLAYING THE GAME.

_____

_____

_____

_____

_____

_____

_____

_____

_____

_____

_____

CREATE A COMIC ABOUT YOUR STORY.

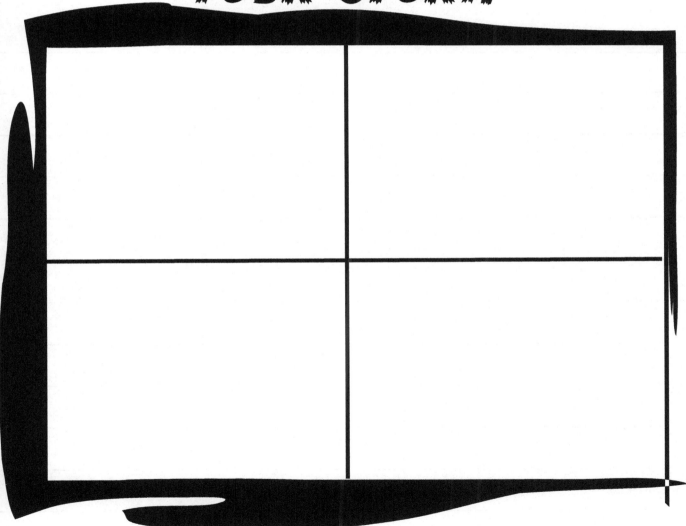

IT IS BECOMING NIGHT AND YOU MUST FIND SHELTER. YOU ONLY HAVE AN AXE IN YOUR INVENTORY...

_____

_____

_____

_____

_____

_____

_____

_____

_____

_____

DRAW A PICTURE TO GO WITH YOUR STORY.

YOU HAVE BUILT A HOUSE WITH A POOL. SUDDENLY THE POOL IS OVERFLOWING WITH WATER. WHAT HAPPENED? CAN YOU FIX IT? HOW?

_____

_____

_____

_____

_____

_____

_____

_____

_____

_____

WHAT IS YOUR FAVORITE THING ABOUT MINECRAFT? WHY DO YOU ENJOY IT SO MUCH?

_____

_____

_____

_____

_____

_____

_____

_____

_____

_____

CREATE A COMIC ABOUT YOUR STORY.

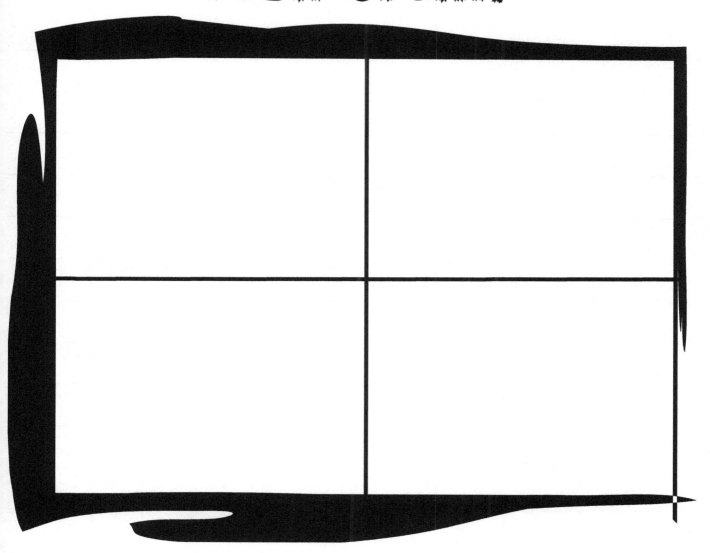

Describe three Minecraft tools and explain how you like to use them. What tool is your favorite to use?

_____

_____

_____

_____

_____

_____

_____

_____

_____

_____

DRAW A PICTURE TO GO WITH YOUR STORY.

YOU ARE GETTING HUNGRY. YOU HAVE NO FOOD IN YOUR INVENTORY. YOU NEED FOOD FAST SO YOU...

_____

_____

_____

_____

_____

_____

_____

_____

_____

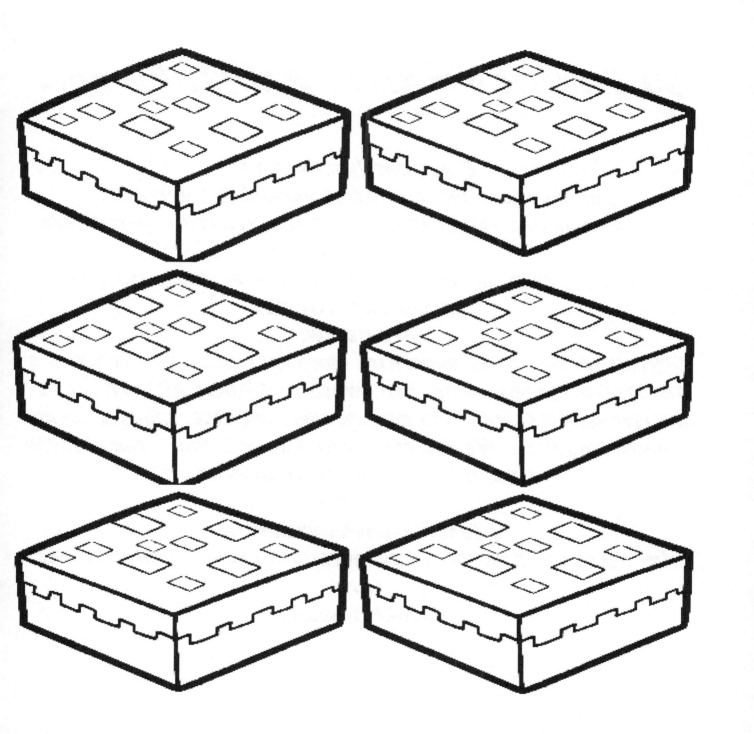

50 Creative Minecraft Writing Prompts

Made in the USA
Monee, IL
26 January 2022

89988487R00059